*M*otivating and *M*obilizing *M*en for *M*inistry

ESTABLISHING AND MAINTAINING AN EFFECTIVE MEN'S MINISTRY IN THE LOCAL CHURCH

Ernest D. Tinsley

SECOND EDITION

Foreword By: Dr. Warren H. Stewart, Sr.

"Motivating and Mobilizing Men For Ministry"

Bullseye Ministries
4 Mancuso Drive
Ossining, NY 10562
info@bullseyeministries.com

Printed in the United States of America

Unless otherwise noted, all scripture quotations
are from the King James Version of the Bible.

For more information, please visit our website:
www.bullseyeministries.com

Foreword

God be praised for this welcomed, refreshing, practical and pointed book entitled **MOTIVATING AND MOBILIZING MEN FOR MINISTRY.** It fulfills its author's purpose of providing an easy-to-read guidebook for pastors, other clergy and laymen to establish and develop a sustained men's ministry in the local church. The author, brother Ernest D. Tinsley, united with the First Institutional Baptist Church of Phoenix, Arizona in 1980 when we both were much younger. He was an energetic, ambitious fresh-out-of-law school attorney who saw our congregation as a socially acceptable organization that would assist him in establishing himself as a reputable professional in the rapidly growing Valley of the Sun. Thank God, Ernest had a life-changing encounter with *"the Author and Finisher of our faith"* and he has never been the same since.

Over the years, Brother Tinsley's personal Lord and Savior has led him through a maturing and pruning process that has transformed him from an aggressive office-holder in the church to *a persuasive and effective Christian leader of men*, not only in the First Institutional Baptist Church, but on the association, state convention and national levels of the National Baptist Convention, USA, Inc. He has served in numerous ministries at his home church, including our Trustees, Deacons, Church School, Christian Studies Institute, Prison and Men of Praise Ministries respectively, as well as provided valuable input for First Institutional's four-phase, VISION 2000 Master Plan which will ultimately result in our completing the construction of an over $8,000,000.00 church campus. Of course, Ernest D. Tinsley's *most significant contribution* to the multifaceted ministry of the congregation where I have served since 1977 is his *leadership of our Men's Ministry* to which he was appointed by this senior pastor.

It is with thanksgiving to God that I attest that our relationship as pastor-to-lay leader has grown over the years to one characterized by mutual respect, genuine appreciation and brotherly love. Therefore, I commend Brother Ernest D. Tinsley for allowing the Lord to use his gifts and talents through discipline and determination to write this valuable manual for Men's Ministry in the local church. May our Lord Jesus Christ richly bless you and your work as you read and share with others the contents of *MOTIVATING AND MOBILIZING MEN FOR MINISTRY.*

Growing in Grace,

Warren H. Stewart, Sr., Senior Pastor
First Institutional Baptist Church
Phoenix, Arizona

About the Author

Ernest D. Tinsley is a member of the First Institutional Baptist Church in Phoenix, Arizona. Over the years he has served his church in a number of capacities, including Deacon, Trustee, Adult Sunday School Superintendent, Evangelism Instructor, Adult Church School Teacher, and coordinator of the Men's Ministry.

In addition, Deacon Tinsley has served as president of the Central District Laymen's Association and of Paradise Baptist State Laymen's Movement. Currently he serves in the National Baptist Laymen's Movement in the following capacities:

Instructor, Allen Jordan Senior and Junior Laymen Seminar;

Director, National Initiative, Development of the Local Church Men's Ministry.

Also, Deacon Tinsley has served as a workshop facilitator and Men's Day speaker at churches and conferences throughout the country.

Recently, Deacon Tinsley formed Bullseye Ministries, which is dedicated to hitting the mark in providing education and edification to Christian men.

Deacon Tinsley, is the father of two daughters, Tiara and Jacqueline, and the husband of Joice Tinsley.

Acknowledgment

To the men of First Institutional Baptist Church, who have allowed me to provide them with leadership over the past twenty years.

To my pastor, Dr. Warren H. Stewart, Sr., who has encouraged me, nurtured the gift in me, and allowed me to exercise that gift under his leadership. Also, special thanks to Dr. Stewart for graciously agreeing to write the Foreword for this book.

To Pastor Ricky Hicks and Sister Donna Johnson for their encouragement, input and editing skills.

To Sis. Sarah Alexander for her excellent transcription skills.

To Sis. Marion Holmes, Sis Nancy Hooper, Bro. Andre Traynham, and Messenger Publishing, LLC for helping to make this dream a reality.

Finally, to God be the glory, for using us in spite of our shortcomings and who called me to this work.

Ernest D. Tinsley

Table of Contents

Introduction

The question reverberates through almost every church: "Where are the men?" The answer is multi-faceted: They are at home, on the golf course, at the ballgame, or at the office. They are running errands and completing chores. Seemingly they are everywhere but the church.

They are also in the church, but they are in the pews, dormant, inactive and ineffective. They make up a vast pool of untapped potential, an army without training or arms. What pastor has not envisioned how the church's ministry could be enhanced if the men of the church could be encouraged and engaged?

An effective men's ministry can serve as the vehicle by which men can be evangelized into Christ and the church and then edified into becoming all that God designed them to be. While many churches have a men's group of some sort, these groups do not always enhance the ministry of the church. By whatever name (Brotherhood, Laymen, Men's Ministry) they are known, these groups often degenerate into an ineffective bible study, or worse a social club dedicated to "fellowship" through "meeting, eating, and greeting." A men's group dedicated to meals, fishing, and bowling is not likely to be effective in "conforming men to the image of God's son".

The purpose of this book is to assist pastors and church leaders in establishing and maintaining an effective local church men's ministry. The concepts described and suggested in the chapters of this book have withstood the test of time and have proved effective in building a men's ministry.

Purpose and Vision are essential in establishing any effective ministry in the church. Chapters I, II, and III discuss how these inter-related concepts provide the foundation and goals for the ministry and determine the organization, function, and design of the ministry. A clear understanding of purpose and vision, coupled with a compatible organizational structure, can prevent aimless activity and fruitless function.

While each local church men's ministry should reflect the vision of that local church, there are some bedrock principles which should be incorporated into every ministry. Those principles are discussed in the remaining chapters of this book. Every men's ministry should be in the business of (1) Drawing men to Christ, (2) Developing men in Christ, and (3) Deploying men for Christ. It is hard to imagine a Christ-centered men's ministry involved in an activity that does not fall within one of these three categories.

Jesus drew men to him. Those men drew other men. (Recall Andrew going to find his brother Simon in order to introduce him to Jesus.) A local church men's ministry should be in the business of continuing this tradition by intentionally designing mechanisms by which men can be drawn to Christ and to the ministry. Chapter IV discusses methods of drawing men.

Jesus developed, and the men He drew to Him developed. Christian men are in dire need of developing into mature disciples who are both F.A.T. (faithful, available, and trainable), and R.E.D. (resilient, effective, and dependable). Chapter V discusses formal methods of developing men; Chapter VI distills from the Proverbs text "iron sharpens iron" several principles for informal development.

Men are action oriented. They equate activity with usefulness. A local church men's ministry can tap into this natural affinity by deploying men into viable and valuable ministries. Jesus deployed men. During the course of His earthly ministry He sent men out on a variety of assignments. And, at the conclusion of His earthly ministry He deployed every Christian – Go ye therefore and teach all nations....

While deployment is essential, it cannot be haphazard. The men's ministry should provide men with a variety of ministry opportunities that will allow a man to work in an area in which he can use his God-given gifts. We all know square pegs do not belong in round holes, but sometimes we place blame in the wrong area. The square peg cannot be faulted; it was designed to be square. Similarly, the round hole cannot be blamed; it was designed to be round. The fault lies with the one who attempted to stick a square peg into a round hole. Chapter VIII discusses how the ministry can assist men in discovering their gifts and finding their God-designed and God-given places in the kingdom of God, and thus avoid deploying men in places for which they were not designed.

Men can be are motivated. Men can be mobilized. An effective men's ministry can provide the arena for men to "step up to the plate" and fulfill their roles within the ministry of the church. It is the hope and prayer of the author that this book will serve as a tool to assist local churches in developing a men's ministry that will enhance the lives of men, expand the ministry of the church, and bring glory to God.

CHAPTER I

Purpose of a Men's Ministry

One lazy Saturday morning I watched my teenage daughter prepare a late breakfast. As I read the morning paper I observed her pouring cereal and milk into a bowl. She then reached into the silverware drawer only to discover that all of the spoons were in the dishwasher. Instead of retrieving a spoon and washing it for her use, she rummaged in the silverware drawer until she came up with what she deemed a suitable substitute. Removing the ice-cream scoop from the drawer, she sat down to eat her bowl of cereal.

As I observed her attempting to use the ice-cream scoop to maneuver cereal and milk from bowl to mouth, two enduring truths about "purpose" were indelibly burned upon my brain:

1. Use of a product outside of its intended purpose is ineffective; and

2. One who uses a product outside of its intended purpose will look silly.

After contemplating my daughter's experiment with the ice-cream scoop, I scavenged around in the back of the silverware drawer and discovered a utensil that was foreign to me. I could not fathom its purpose, but instinctively knew that it must have had a purpose at one time. Later, I showed the utensil to my wife, who explained that it was a tea ball used to steep loose tealeaves in hot water in order to make fresh brewed tea. Had my wife not revealed to me the purpose of the tea ball, it would have remained unused in the back of our silverware drawer.

Purpose exists whether it is known or hidden. That the tea ball's purpose was unknown to me did not mean that it did not have a purpose. In order for a product to be used properly, however, its purpose must be known. Revealed purpose also provides understanding of the use and potential of a product.

Conversely, unknown purpose leads to misuse, abuse, lack of use, and reduction in function. In a pinch, a wrench can probably be used to drive a nail. Such use, however, will damage the wrench, and is much less effective than using a hammer to accomplish the task.

Purpose is the driving force behind creation. Nothing has ever been created without a purpose in mind. As the ultimate creator, God initiated the relationship between creation and purpose in Chapter 1 of the book of Genesis.

Verses	**Creation**	**Purpose**
3-5	Light and Darkness	Creation of the first day
6	Firmament	Divide the waters from the waters
9	Gathered waters	Appearance of dry land
11	Fruit trees	To yield fruit after its kind
14-18	Light	Rule over the day, and over the night

| 20-22 | Moving creatures, fowl | Be fruitful, multiply, fill the waters and the seas |
| 26 | Man | To have dominion over everything |

Notice that every time God created something, He declared its purpose. God made His purpose known so that everything He created could be used properly, its value and potential fully appreciated.

Individuals are no exception; every man, every woman was created with a purpose in mind. Those who understand, accept and labor within their divinely created purpose are most effective in ministry and in life.

The Apostle Paul was acutely aware of his purpose. As he concluded his farewell letter to Timothy, Paul declared his readiness to die and expressed satisfaction that he had finished his course. *"For I am now ready to be offered, and the time of my departure is at hand. I have fought a good fight, I have finished my* course, I have kept the faith." (II Timothy 4:6-7). In an earlier letter he declared that he ran his race with certainty and fought his fight strategically and with conviction. *"Do you not know that in a race all the runners compete, but only one receives the prize? So run that you may obtain it. Every athlete exercises self-control in all things. They do it to receive a perishable wreath, but we an imperishable. Well, I do not run aimlessly, I do not box as one beating the air, but I pommel my body and subdue it, lest after preaching to others I myself should be disqualified." (I Corinthians 9:24-26 RSV).* Paul's success, effectiveness, and fruitfulness as a disciple were due in large part to his understanding and appreciation of his purpose as defined by his "course" and his "race".

Jesus was also aware of His purpose. In numerous scriptures Jesus declared both the "what" of His purpose and "how" it would be accomplished.

5

WHAT

"I am come that they might have life, and that they might have it more abundantly." *(John 10:10)*

"For I came down from Heaven, not to do mine own will, but the will of Him that sent me." (John 6:38)

"Think not that I am come to destroy the law, or the prophets: I am not come to destroy, but to fulfill." (Matthew 5:17)

"For the Son of Man is come to seek and to save that which was lost." (Luke 19:10)

HOW

"The Spirit of the Lord is upon me, because He hath anointed me to preach the gospel to the poor; He hath sent me to heal the brokenhearted, to preach deliverance to the captives, and recovery of sight to the blind, to set at liberty them that are bruised, to preach the acceptable year of the Lord." (Luke 4:18-19)

"For even the Son of Man came not to be ministered unto, but to minister, and to given His life a ransom for many." (Mark 10:45)

ORGANIZATIONAL PURPOSE

Like individuals, organizations should have a known purpose. KFC, formerly known as Kentucky Fried Chicken, the well-known fast food retailer, has a well-defined and equally well-articulated purpose: "We Do Chicken Right." This statement of purpose has several exemplary effects.

1. It focuses its employees on themes of teamwork ("we"), action ("do") singularity ("chicken"), and quality ("right").

2. It alerts potential customers to these same attributes.

3. It serves to distinguish KFC from other fast-food retailers who sell a variety of foods. For better or for worse, everybody knows and understands that if you go to KFC, you will be eating chicken.

A local church men's ministry should have a similarly well-defined purpose. That purpose should come from God, through the pastor, and through the leadership of the men's ministry. In the absence of a clearly understood purpose, the ministry is destined to aimless activity and ineffective efforts. That purpose should be reflected in the ministry's statement of vision.

CHAPTER II

Vision for a Men's Ministry

Vision is an essential prerequisite to any movement of any aspect of the Church. *"Where there is no vision, the people perish." (Proverbs 29:18a).* A ministry without vision is destined to die.

What is a vision? The Hebrew word translated "vision" in the quoted text literally means *revelation.* Through visions God conveys to His people His will and His specific plan for their future. Thus, we can understand a vision as "a glimpse of God's plan."

The New International Version translation of Proverbs 29:18a provides additional insight into the benefits of a properly received and understood vision. *"Where there is no revelation, the people cast off restraint."* A properly understood vision restrains a people from deviating from the course God has ordained for them. Many churches and many ministries within churches have "perished" or are on life support because they strayed from the fruitful path God had ordained.

God conveys His vision to His people effectively and orderly. Daniel's experience is enlightening.

> *In the third year of Cyrus, king of Persia, a thing was revealed unto Daniel, whose name was called Belteshazzar; and the thing was true, but the time appointed was long: and he understood the thing and had understanding of the vision . . . . Then I lifted up mine eyes, and looked, and behold a certain man clothed in linen, whose loins were girded with fine gold of Uphaz; his body also was like the beryl, and his face as the appearance of lightning, and his eyes as lamps of fire, and his arms and his feet like in color to polished brass, and the voice of his words like the voice of a multitude. And I Daniel alone saw the vision: for the men that were with me saw not the vision; but a great quaking fell upon them so that they fled to hide themselves. " (Daniel 10:1, 5-7)*

Note the bedrock truth revealed in Daniel's account. The vision came to him and to him alone. Although others were in his presence at the time of the vision, none saw what Daniel saw. In fact, the experience frightened the other men to the point that they ran and hid.

There are several significant implications from God's methodology of providing his vision only to his chosen leader:

  1. It is essential that every movement of the church be led by the person God ordained for that position.

Unfortunately, many churches choose leaders, including the pastor, without seeking God's choice for the position. In selecting leaders we often rely upon resumes and relationships instead of revelation. Many churches and numerous ministries within churches are dead and aimless because they are led by someone other than God's chosen leader.

  2. The leader God has called must be ever vigilant to understand God's vision for the ministry.

The secular skills the leader brings to the position may be helpful *if* employed in conjunction with and in deference to *God's vision* for the ministry.

> 3. Members of the ministry must defer to the leader's understanding and explanation of the vision.

In His infinite wisdom God has determined not to provide His vision to every member of the ministry. Thus, members often are placed in the position of following a leader who is following a vision that the followers have not seen and do not understand. The deacon who declares that he does not see the pastor's vision is more correct than he knows.

Similarly, a ministry member may not understand the vision of the ministry leader. In *John 14*, the Disciples revealed their lack of understanding of the vision God had given Jesus. *"Thomas said to him, Lord, we do not know where you are going: How can we know the way?"* *(John 14:5 RSV)* Like Thomas, there will be many

12

followers who neither know nor understand where their leader is going. The test of good "follow-ship" is to exhibit the faith to follow even when the follower does not understand where the leader is going.

BENEFITS OF KNOWING THE VISION

The bible delineates at least four specific benefits of knowing and understanding God's vision.

(1)   **Assignment** - God assigns specific tasks to His people through visions. Paul's experience on the Damascus Road is a prime example:

> *"And as he journeyed he came near Damascus: and suddenly there shined around about him a light from heaven: and he fell to the earth and heard a voice saying unto him, Saul, Saul, why persecutest thou me? And he said who art thou, Lord? And the Lord said I am Jesus whom though persecutest: it is hard for thee to kick against the pricks. And he trembling and astonished said, Lord, what wilt thou have me to do? And the Lord said unto him, arise, and go into the city, and it shall be told thee what thou must do." Acts 9:3-6*

(2)   **Encouragement** - In Genesis Chapter 15 Abraham was bemoaning his childlessness. In a vision, God encouraged him with these words:

> *After these things, the Word of the Lord came unto Abram in a vision, saying, fear not, Abram: I am thy shield and thy exceeding great reward. And Abram said Lord God, what wilt thou give me, seeing I go childless, and the steward of my house is this Ellezer of Damascus? And Abram said Behold, to me thou hast given no seed: and lo, one born in my house is mine heir. And, behold, the Word of the Lord came unto him, saying, This shall not be thine heir; but he that shall come forth out of thine own bowels shall be thine heir. (Genesis 15:1-4)*

(3)   **Instruction** - In *Ezekiel 37: 1-14* God provided Ezekiel with a vision of a valley full of dry bones. In that vision God gave Ezekiel several specific instructions to demonstrate God's ability to resurrect His people despite their apparent dire circumstances. Specifically, God instructed Ezekiel to pass by the bones (verse 2); prophesy to the bones (verse 4); prophesy to the wind (verse 9); and prophesy to the children of Israel (verses 12-14).

(4)   **Specific Guidance** - In a vision recounted in *Acts 18:9-10,* God gave Paul specific instructions to remain in Corinth and to continue preaching despite his frustrations with the people's response. Later, in **Acts 22:17-21,** God specifically instructed Paul to leave Jerusalem.

These general biblical truths concerning vision have specific application to the men's ministry in a local church:

(1)   A vision is necessary to the fruitfulness of the men's ministry.

(2)   God will give His vision for the ministry to the man He has called to lead the ministry.

(3)   The ministry must select as its leader the man God has designed for that position and then follow him faithfully.

Through visions God will provide the people with a leader, and through the leader He will provide the people with assignments, encouragement, instruction, and specific guidance.

THE PASTOR'S ROLE

As ultimate earthly leader it is the pastor's responsibility to articulate a vision for the church and for each ministry in the church. God gave these instructions to Habakkuk with respect to the vision God had given him for the people.

> "And the Lord answered me, and said, write the vision, and make it plain upon tables, that he may run that readeth it."
> (*Habakkuk 2:2*)

For a men's ministry to be effective, the ministry leader must first understand the vision God has given the pastor for the church. That leader then must seek God's vision for the men's ministry. Obviously, any vision God gives a ministry leader within a church will be consistent with the vision God has given the pastor for the entire church. No men's ministry can be fruitful unless it is working within the "restraints" of the vision God has given the pastor for the church.

GOD'S CALL OF A LEADER

God's call of a leader is normally direct and private. His call of Gideon, found in Judges 6, provides several insights into the process.

(1)   God called Gideon while he was busy carrying out his earthly father's instructions. ***Judges 6:11-14.***

(2)   Gideon felt unworthy of the call God had placed upon his life. The actual language is revealing:

"Oh my* Lord, *wherewith shall I save Israel? Behold, my family is poor in Manasseh, and I am the least in my father's house." (Judges 6:15)

Are there men in your church who are more confident in their own abilities than in God's ability to use them? Under the Gideon model, such men are not currently candidates for leadership in the church.

(3)   On at least three occasions Gideon requested reassurance that he was being called by the one and true God.

In ***Judges 6:17,*** Gideon specifically asked for a sign. In response, God instructed Gideon to lay a calf and unleavened cakes upon a rock, whereupon the Lord touched the calf and bread with the end of his staff and caused a spontaneous combustion. Not being satisfied, Gideon made his well-known demands that God first wet a piece of fleece while keeping the ground dry, and then wet the ground while keeping dry a second piece of fleece. *Judges 6:36-40*. On each occasion God did what Gideon requested. (See Chapter VIII of this book for an expanded discussion of this event.)

Gideon's requests for reassurance demonstrate his unwillingness to accept an assignment without being convinced that he was working in concert with the Almighty. God's willingness to provide Gideon with reassurance, even to the point of acquiescing in seemingly silly requests, demonstrates God's determination to use His selected leader irrespective of the leader's initial reluctance. And, as we know, Gideon went on to lead the people of Israel to a great and decisive victory against the enemies of the children of God (Judges 7).

A MAN' S VISION FOR HIMSELF

Before leaving this vital topic we must say a word about the importance of a man having a proper vision for himself. In *Isaiah 6:1-8*, the prophet recounts the vision he received from God "in the year King Uzziah died." This four-fold vision enabled Isaiah to fulfill the call God had on his life:

(1)   *A vision of God* - In verses 1-4 Isaiah describes in vivid detail his vision of the Almighty God. He was "high and lifted up" and "His train filled the temple". Six-winged seraphims serenaded God with cries of Holy, Holy, Holy, in response to which the post of the door moved and the house filled with smoke. Gideon's vision began with a view of the awesomeness of God.

(2)   *A vision of self* - Having encountered the Almighty, Isaiah's mind immediately moved to a vision of himself. (v.5) In that vision he saw both his own uncleanliness and the uncleanliness of the people in his community. In other words, like Gideon, Isaiah was overwhelmed with a sense of his own unworthiness, and again, like Gideon, this sense of

19

unworthiness put Isaiah right in position to be used by God.

(3)   *A vision of God's grace* - In verses 6 and 7 Isaiah saw one of the seraphim take a live coal from the altar, lay it upon Isaiah's mouth, and declare "Lo, this hath touched thy lips; and thine iniquity is taken away, and thy sin purged." Having acknowledged his own unworthiness, Isaiah then received symbolic cleansing from the altar of God, just as Christians receive cleansing through the saving grace and purifying blood of Jesus Christ.

(4)   *A vision of ability* - (v. 8) Having been purged, Isaiah now was ready to accept whatever assignment God had for him. The reader is no doubt familiar with God's inquiry and Isaiah's response: "And I heard the voice of the Lord, saying, Whom shall I send, and who will go for us? Then said I, here am I; send me."

Through visions given to the pastor, to the leader of the men's ministry, and to individual men, a successful and fruitful men's ministry can develop men who recognize God's omnipotence, their own inadequacy, God's saving grace, and their ability, in God and through the help of the Holy Spirit, to do whatever God assigns to their hands.

CHAPTER III

Function, Design, and Organization

The purpose of an organization is revealed in its vision. Purpose determines function, which in turn dictates design. The ice-cream scoop employed by my daughter to eat cereal is instructive of this relationship. The scoop has a strong, thick handle and a deep, wide scoop. The entire instrument is made of a durable material and the handle has grooves.

This design permits the scoop to be used to dig out frozen ice cream. (In converse to my oldest daughter, my youngest daughter once used a soupspoon to scoop ice cream. She broke the spoon because its handle was too thin to withstand the force generated by attempting to scoop out hard, frozen ice cream.) If you lay an ice cream scoop and a soupspoon side-by-side, through analysis of their respective designs you can determine their individual purposes. This analysis holds true with respect to the simplest object, such as spoons and ice cream scoops, as well as the most complicated computer chips or rocket engines.

Computer programmers are familiar with the relationship between purpose, function, and design. Every computer program begins with a purpose. For instance, a business owner might desire to computerize his or her inventory tracking system. To do so the owner would inform the computer programmer of his or her purpose and of the manner in which the store handles its inventory. With that information the programmer could design a program that is compatible with the store's function and suitable for the owner's purpose.

Consider the function and design of the dispute-resolution system Jethro recommended to Moses *(Exodus 18:13-24)*. Jethro noticed that Moses spent all day everyday deciding disputes between the people. The disputes were many, and the line to see Moses was long.

After hearing Moses' explanation of his procedure, Jethro advised Moses that his method of resolving disputes would wear out both Moses and the people (v. 18). Jethro then suggested a system that was designed to fulfill Moses' purpose and benefit both Moses and the people:

1. Moses remained the sole spokesman for the people towards God (v. 19);

2. Moses was to instruct the people in the law and their conduct (v. 20);

3. Moses was to appoint assistants to help him judge disputes (v. 21);

4. Small matters would be judged by the assistants; Moses would continue to judge the more serious disputes (v. 22);

5. The new system would ease the burden on both Moses and the people: Moses no longer was required to hear every case, and the people no longer were required to wait on line hour after hour to have their dispute heard (v. 23).

Perhaps most importantly, Moses saw the wisdom of Jethro's suggestion and implemented Jethro's design (v. 24).

In the New Testament, God provides an organizational chart to facilitate the work of the church. *"And his gifts were that some should be apostles, some profits, some evangelists, some pastors and teachers, to equip the saints for the work of ministry, for building up the body of Christ, until we all attain to the unity of the faith and of the knowledge of the son of God, to mature manhood, to the measure of the stature of the fullness of Christ; so that we may no longer be children, tossed to and fro and carried about with every wind of doctrine, by the cunning of men, by there craftiness in deceitful wiles. Rather, speaking the truth and love, we are to grow up in every way into him who is the head, into Christ, from whom the whole body, joined and knit together by every joint with which is supplied, when each part is working properly, makes bodily growth and up builds its self in love (Ephesians 4:11-16).*

Note the salient points derived from this text:

1. God provides specially gifted individuals (apostles, prophets, evangelists, pastor-teachers) to the Church;

2. These specially gifted individuals are provided to equip the members of the church (the saints);

3. Once equipped, the saints are to perform the work of the ministry;

4. When the church functions within these guidelines, it will experience at least seven benefits:

    a. Unity of the faith

    b. Knowledge of the Son of God

    c. Maturity

    d. Stability

    e. Loving speech

    f. Christ-like members

    g. Integrated function

Similarly, the design of a men's ministry in the local church should reflect the purpose of the ministry and the intended function of its component parts. For instance (and we do not advocate this), suppose a men's ministry existed solely for the purpose of providing married men and their wives with opportunities for social outings. The design of that ministry might include an individual to coordinate publicity, another to coordinate ticket sales, and a third to select events. That ministry would have no need for a Bible Study Coordinator, Evangelism Outreach Director, or any of the other positions which would be required if the ministry's purpose included those activities.

The purpose of the Men's Ministry at the author's church, as expressed in its vision, is "Drawing, Developing, and Deploying Men for the Cause of Christ." The design of the ministry reflects that purpose. Attached, as Appendix 1, is a copy of the organization chart of that ministry. Notice the following from the design of the ministry:

(1) The Men's Ministry falls under the guidance of the Holy Spirit, the Church, and the Pastor.

(2) The Men's Ministry has one leader who is responsible for providing vision for the ministry and leadership to the ministry, all under the leadership and guidance of the Pastor.

(3) The leader has a staff of assistants who coordinate Bible studies, information (the secretary), new member follow-up, prayer, and special events.

(4) The Men's Ministry consists of five separate ministries, each with its own leader. Each of these five ministries falls under the leadership of the Men's Ministry leader.

(5) Consistent with the vision of the Church, the Men's Ministry evangelism ministry is the most prominent ministry in the organization.

Again, it is emphatically not the intent of this book to suggest that the design of the Men's Ministry at the author's church is the best or most efficient design. It is simply presented as an example of how one Men's

Ministry is designed consistent with the purpose and vision of the Men's Ministry and of the local church of which it is a part. Every men's ministry should be custom designed to meet the purpose and vision of its pastor and church.

FTBC MEN'S MINISTRY ORGANIZATIONAL CHART

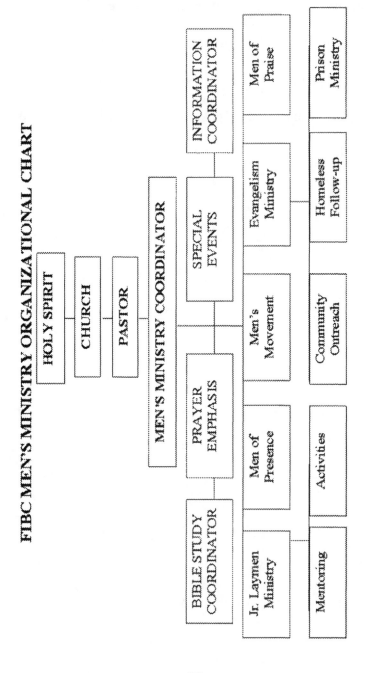

Appendix 1

CHAPTER IV

Drawing Men

Every men's ministry should employ mechanisms designed to draw men to the ministry, the church, and Jesus Christ. A ministry made up of born-again, spirit-filled men is uniquely qualified to present the Gospel and the person of Jesus Christ to unsaved and unchurched men. In *I Corinthians 9:20-23*, Paul described his technique of identifying with the various targets of his evangelistic effort. *"To the Jew I became like a Jew. ... To those under the law I became like one under the law. ... To the weak I became weak. ... I have become all things to all men so that by all possible means I might save some."*

Jesus declared that if His followers would lift Him, He would draw all men unto Himself (**John 12:32**). A men's ministry can lift Jesus in at least three ways:

31

(1) *Lift His Word* - The Word of God must be the centerpiece of any ministry in the church, including a men's ministry. Men-only Bible studies are uniquely able to draw men in that they allow men to express themselves more candidly than they might when they are in the presence of women. Over time bonds also will develop between the men who attend such Bible studies.

(2) *Lift His Work* - A men's ministry should be focused on the work of Jesus. That work includes evangelism, discipleship, and the "helps" ministries listed by Jesus in *Matthew 25:35-40,* (visiting the sick, visiting those in prison, feeding the hungry, etc.). Many men's ministries miss the mark in this aspect of the work. A ministry that is focused solely inward, without any outreach effort, is doomed to stagnation and ineffectiveness. A men's ministry is not a social club, although it has social aspects. If it is to be a true ministry, it must reach outside of its own concentric circle of convenience and touch those who are in need of the grace, mercy, and power of Jesus Christ.

(3) *Lift His Way* - A men's ministry can lift Jesus by cultivating men who exemplify a Christ-like lifestyle.

This concept will be developed further in Chapter V of this book. For now, suffice it to say that when one brother counsels another brother about an aspect in that brother's lifestyle, he is lifting Jesus and will draw either that man closer to Jesus, or he will draw others who will be impressed and enticed by the lifestyle and commitment of the stronger brother.

At the church where the author serves as coordinator of the Men's Ministry, there are numerous activities and efforts designed to draw men to the Ministry. The following list is by no means exhaustive, but rather suggestive of different methodologies of drawing men to the Ministry.

(1) *Monthly Breakfast* - On the first Saturday of every month the Men's Ministry holds a breakfast at a local restaurant (the restaurant is owned by a member of the church who makes the restaurant available to the Men's Ministry and charges a very reasonable price for the breakfast). The agenda for the breakfast includes a devotional period, breakfast, sometimes a musical selection from the male chorus, and then a 15 to 20-minute message from

one of the members of the Ministry or a special guest. After the message, first time visitors are welcomed, and then brief (2-3 minute) presentations are made about upcoming events and ongoing ministry opportunities. Thus, the breakfast provides opportunity for fellowship, sharing in the Word, and recruitment.

(2) *Monthly Letter* - The Men's Ministry sends a monthly letter to every man in the church who has shown even the slightest interest in any aspect of the ministry. The letter goes out eight days prior to the monthly breakfast and serves both as a reminder of the breakfast and as an additional method of providing information to the brothers regarding upcoming ministry opportunities, events, and activities.

(3) *New Member Tracking* - The author's home church disciples new members individually after they join the church. The discipleship process includes a personally assigned disciplemaker and four new members' classes. The Men's Ministry supplements this discipleship ministry by contacting directly each new man, inviting him to the next monthly breakfast, and informing him of the ministry opportunities available to him. The goal is to lead every new man into participating in one of the several ministries that operate under

34

the umbrella of the Men's Ministry. Once a man expresses an interest in a specific ministry, he is turned over to that ministry for continued follow-up and discipleship.

(4) *"Feeder Ministries"* - As outlined in Chapter 3, our Men's Ministry includes both a male chorus and an all-male usher ministry. There are some men who for a variety of reasons are drawn directly to one of these two ministries. In the past, these ministries would have been satisfied to have received a new member. Now, however, with the concept of a comprehensive men's ministry, the male chorus and the male ushers act as "feeder ministries" into the broader men's ministry. Any man who joins one of these ministries is added to the mailing list, begins receiving the monthly newsletter, receives invitations to the monthly breakfast, and is made aware of the other ministry opportunities available to him.

(5) *Fellowship Outings* - Fellowship outings can be an effective tool in development of a Christ-centered Men's Ministry. They can also become the tail that wags the dog. Such outings are most effective when they are planned with a purpose and focused by the vision of the ministry. In fact, one of the more effective men involved

in the Men's Ministry at the author's home church was drawn during a bowling outing. He had heard numerous announcements about the monthly breakfast, but had not responded. He had been invited at least a few times, but had not come. However, when he heard that the men were going on a bowling outing, he signed up. At the outing he discovered that the men involved in the Men's Ministry were not stuck-up, walking-on water, holier-than-thou "saints", but rather were a compilation of ordinary men not unlike himself. From that outing he began coming to the monthly breakfast, and since that time has served as the president of the male chorus, financial secretary of the Men's Ministry, and co-coordinator of the Junior Laymen Ministry.

(6) *Annual Retreat* - Retreats provide an opportunity for renewal and recruiting. The renewal and refreshing aspects of a retreat are well known. Less well known is the opportunity for recruitment. The man who currently serves as general secretary of our Men's Ministry ignored invitations to the monthly breakfast and other invitations to participate for years. However, for a reason known only to him and to God, he signed up for and attended our first annual retreat and was drawn to the Men's Ministry by

what he experienced during that weekend. He asked what he could do to help the ministry, and with his computer skills and meticulous nature he fit right in as the secretary of the Ministry.

There are doubtless numerous other methods by which men can be drawn to the ministry. The point is that every men's ministry ought to purposely and intentionally develop methodologies that draw men to the ministry for the ultimate purpose of developing them and deploying them for the cause of Christ.

CHAPTER V

Developing Men

Every Christian is in need of constant development. Each of us is in the process of being *"conformed to the image of [Jesus]" (Romans 8:29).* Even Jesus developed. The second chapter of Luke's Gospel describes how Jesus increased in wisdom (verse 40) and stature (verse 52). He did so by, among other things, studying with the learned men of his day (verse 46).

Paul encouraged Timothy to develop. In *II Timothy 1:6* Paul instructed Timothy to stir up the gift that was inside of him. Like Timothy, every man has a gift lying within him that is in need of "stirring" or developing. *Roman 12:6.* Paul also encouraged Timothy to develop by studying so that he could become an approved workman. *II Timothy 2:15.*

Paul also encouraged the church at Ephesus, and by extrapolation admonished all of the members of the Body of Christ, to develop via a four-fold process:

- Put off the old man *(Ephesians 4:22)*

- Be renewed in your spirit *(Ephesians 4:23)*

- Put on the new man *(Ephesians 4:24)*

- Put on the whole armor of God *(Ephesians 6:10-18)*

The men's ministry in any local church should foster and promote an atmosphere of development. In every meeting of every arm of the Men's Ministry in our church we stress the need for continuing development. We rely upon the dynamic of positive peer pressure to encourage men to become active Bible students and active participants in other developmental activities. Every man is encouraged to be an active member of a church-sponsored communal Bible study, whether it is a Church School class or some other Bible study offered by the church. Our Men's Ministry also offers a men-only Bible study on Sunday morning during the Church School hour where we discuss topics directly relevant to the lives of men. We sponsor workshops and seminars for the same purpose and periodically schedule outings to workshops and seminars held by other local and national organizations.

We have also discovered that Christian growth can be fostered through the development of interpersonal relationships between brothers. There are some who advocate the establishment of formalized small groups in order to achieve this goal. This may work for some, and there is much literature available on this type of ministry. However, we have found that personal relationships are developed best not through formalized small groups, but through the natural bonding that occurs as men study and work together.

When Jesus issued the Great Commission, the first word of which is translated "Go", in *Matthew 28:19*, He used a word that literally means *as you go*. We have come to believe that interpersonal relationships are best developed "as you go", and have discovered that as men go to Bible study, as men go to the prison, as men go to feed the homeless, as men go to retreats and other off-site activities, they naturally and instinctively develop interpersonal relationships.

This natural development of interpersonal relationships, which leads to informal discipline among men, is what the Proverb writer had in mind when he advised that "iron sharpens iron."

CHAPTER VI

Iron Sharpens Iron

Every man wants to be sharp. No man desires to go through life regarded as dull. Sharpness is a highly desirable attribute.

Even when we were in high school we singled out certain individuals as sharp. The student who instantly understood the complex concepts of Calculus, and who was able to remember all of the significant dates and events in World History, was said to have a sharp mind. The fellow who wore the latest fashions and who always kept his shoes polished to a high sheen was said to be a sharp dresser. And the one who combined it all, who had obvious leadership skills, academic acumen, and prowess on the athletic field was simply said to be sharp.

In the secular world, then, sharpness has come to be defined as one who is a cut above, a step ahead. One who has it all together.

Sharpness is also a Christian virtue. You will not find sharpness listed as one of the fruit of the spirit in Galatians 5, nor will you find it as one of the spiritual gifts listed in Romans 12. Nevertheless, all Christians should strive to be a cut above, a step ahead. In fact, Christians are commanded to strive to be like Jesus. *"Let this mind be in you, which also was in Christ Jesus." (Philippians 2:5)*

In *Proverbs 27:17,* we find these words: *"Iron sharpens iron; so a man sharpens the countenance of his friend."* In those few words we find the biblical formula for how to become sharp.

First and foremost, the text implies without stating that men are in need of sharpening. This is a subtle but significant point. No man has ever improved without first recognizing the need for improvement. No man has ever progressed without first becoming dissatisfied with his current condition. Unfortunately, there are many men in our churches who do not feel the need to progress or improve; they are comfortable in their current condition.

I was reminded of men like these one evening while I was washing the dishes after our family dinner. At the time we were the proud owners of a goldfish by the name of Goldie. Goldie lived in a one-gallon fish bowl that sat on a ledge directly above the kitchen sink. As I washed the dishes I began to observe Goldie. I noticed how he would swim from side to side across the surface of the water. Then, presumably for a change of pace, he would swim rapidly in a circle around the perimeter of the bowl. Finally, in a display of boldness, he would dive from the surface of the water to the bottom of the bowl, and then rapidly ascend back to the surface.

He carried on like this for several minutes, doing whatever he pleased, whenever he pleased. For some reason my mind began to wander, and I began to consider what was going on in Goldie's mind. I concluded that he thought he was hot stuff.

After all, he was the strongest fish in the fish bowl, the fastest fish in the fish bowl, the most agile fish in the fish bowl, and no doubt the toughest fish in the fish bowl. Of course, he was the only fish in the fish bowl!

I then began to wonder how Goldie's self-perception would change if his environment was altered. I imagined how he would view himself if, instead of being alone in a one-gallon fish bowl, he found himself swimming with other fish of varying sizes in a 20-gallon aquarium. I then further imagined what would happen to Goldie's self-image were he to be dumped in the ocean with all manner of sharks, whales, and the like. I concluded that if Goldie had a different environment, he would have a different self-image.

So it is with men of the church. Many times our perceptions of ourselves, including our self-image of our level of "sharpness", comes by comparing ourselves to other men of the church. Unfortunately, in many instances that is not a challenging standard. If we become complacent because we are satisfied with the state of our development relative to those we encounter on a daily basis, we will never achieve the potential that God has deposited in us. Like Goldie, we need to come to appreciate that there is a big world out there, that there are men involved in marvelous and magnificent ministries who are having an impact on the lives of people, and that maybe God actually has more in mind for us than counting the offering one Sunday a month, or singing a solo when called upon by the choir director. The ancient proverb says that every journey begins with one step; the first step on the journey to sharpness is a realization of the need to get sharper.

Second, sharpness is a function of contact. For any object to be sharpened, it must be in contact with another object. A knife lying on a counter, by itself, will never get sharp, no matter how much you will it to become sharp.

And so it is with us as men. "No man is an island." Men who disdain the company of other men, men who believe they "have it all together", and do not need to associate with other men in a Christian setting, are doomed to dullness. There is no place for lone wolves in the Christian community. "We are one body, with many members." *Romans 12:4.*

Further, it is not sufficient to simply have contact with any random person. The text says **iron** sharpens iron. In other words, the nature and substance of that with which you have contact is just as important as the contact itself. To continue the knife sharpening analogy, if you were to take a knife and rub it up and down the side of a stick of butter, the knife would never get sharper, again, no matter how much you willed it to be so. In order for the knife to be sharpened, it must be brought into contact with something that is strong, firm, and full of substance.

So it is with us as we attempt to become sharper. Men must seek out other men who are more spiritually mature, more seasoned, and more gifted for the purpose of rubbing against them in labor and fellowship. The Promise Keepers teach that every man ought to have a "Paul" in his life. They are imminently correct. Who is the "Paul" in your life? Who is the man in your life to whom you can turn when you need advice, instruction, or encouragement? If you would be sharp, you need a Paul.

Third, the Proverbs writer points out that sharpening your brother is a friendly act. "Iron sharpens iron, thus does a man sharpen the countenance of his **friend**." This reminder is significant because on many occasions the sharpening process can be a painful process. In a final look at the knife-sharpening analogy, the knife becomes sharper because certain aspects of the blade are cut away. A more apt example may be sharpening a pencil. We have all seen how a pencil sharpener cuts away the wood and portions of the lead, leaving a fine point.

Sharpening men is no different. Each of us has some attitudes and some attributes and some activities that need to be cut away. Over the years they may have grown close to us; severing them may be painful. When we form a relationship with a sharp brother who begins to admonish us in love about a certain attribute, encouraging us to do better and go farther, we may experience pain, which could lead us to conclude that the brother who is trying to sharpen us really is trying to attack us. It is at that moment that we need to be reminded that the sharpening process, no matter how painful, is a friendly act.

Recall if you will David's encounter with Nathan. *II Samuel 12*. David had sinned with Bathsheba and then compounded the sin by conspiring to have Bathsheba's husband killed in battle. In a subsequent conversation, Nathan told David a story about a man who, although the owner of numerous sheep, killed his neighbor's only lamb. Nathan asked David what should be done with the man. David responded that the man ought to be killed. Nathan then looked at David and said sternly, "Thou art the man."

There is no doubt that this was a painful experience for David. He had been confronted not only with an apt characterization of his own sin, but by his own judgment of his just punishment. At that moment it would be well for David to be reminded that Nathan was just being friendly; he was simply attempting to sharpen David by helping him to realize the wrongness of his conduct.

This is why brotherly relationships are so important. We are more apt to accept criticism from a person we trust and in whom we have the confidence that whatever they say or do to us, it is done out of love and for our best, than from a person with whom we do not have such a relationship.

Finally, sharpness will alter every aspect of your life to the point where you will even look different. The text says that sharpness affects our "countenance", which is defined as how we appear. Countenance has more to do with internal attitude than with external features. If we become sharp, our countenance will become bright and joyful. We will look excited about the things in which we are involved, and we will show joy as we labor with Christ.

The positive affects of a sharp countenance will spill over into our personal lives. A man who is fulfilling God's call on his life, who is becoming more like Christ day by day, makes for a much more enjoyable companion than one who is stuck in a spiritual rut. His children will see the change, and will likely become more interested in the church and what it has to offer. There is no aspect of a man's life that will go untouched if he makes the commitment to become sharper in Christ. And, as indicated previously, a men's ministry provides a perfect incubator for the nurturing of the type of relationships that will allow men to help each other reach their potential in Jesus.

CHAPTER VII

Deploying Men

A comprehensive men's ministry will do more than draw men and develop them. It will also deploy them into ministries operated by the men's ministry as well as into ministries operated by the church at-large.

In *Luke 10:1-17* we find an example of Jesus deploying men whom He had been drawn and developed. His methodology is instructive as we fulfill this aspect of the ministry.

Verse 1 - *Jesus appointed 70 men and sent them out*

Notice that Jesus did not send out all of His followers. He chose 70 who, no doubt, had demonstrated their readiness to be deployed. Further note that deployment requires a sending out. Deployment requires leaving the cocoon of the ministry. Men who never step outside of the ministry will never fulfill God's plan for their lives.

Verse 2 - Jesus instructs the 70 to pray for more workers

It appears that Jesus desired to send more than 70 on this mission, but only 70 were ready to be deployed at that time. This should provide comfort to those currently in leadership roles in ministries who have a desire for more workers, as well as instruction on the value of prayer in building a Christ-centered ministry.

Verse 3- Jesus advises the 70 that He is sending them out as lambs among wolves.

Men who are being deployed into outreach ministry need constant reminding of the type of people they will encounter and the attitude they are to maintain during these encounters.

Verse 4 - Jesus instructs the men to stay focused by not carrying a purse, money or shoes, and to salute no man by the way.

Distraction is one of Satan's most effective tools in deterring ministry. Men who are deployed in ministry must be reminded to stay focused on the task at hand.

***Verses 5-9 - <u>Jesus provides the men with instruction on
how to interrelate with the people they encounter while
they are in ministry.</u>***

While it is unlikely that men deployed in a modern
day men's ministry will need to rely upon people along
the way for housing and sustenance, it is important that
men always remember that they represent Jesus with
respect to each individual they encounter along the way.

For instance, the men's ministry at the author's
local church operates a prison ministry. Some of our best
and most significant opportunities to witness occur not
when we interact with the inmates, but when we interact
with the correction officers we encounter "along the
way."

***Verses 10-16 - <u>Jesus instructs the men on handling
rejection.</u>***

Often men who are deployed for the first time are
surprised when they are not universally received. How we
handle rejection is an intricate part of our witness to those
we encounter. Many men become frustrated when their

witnessing efforts do not immediately bear fruit. Paul addresses this concern in *I Corinthians 3:5-6,* where he notes that it is our assignment to plant and to water, and it is up to God to give the increase. In a result-oriented, success-driven world, men must be reminded that in this arena success is determined by whether the effort was Christ-like and effective, not by the immediate result.

Verse 17 - *The Seventy express amazement.*

Upon their return the 70 declared in amazement that even the devils were subject to them. If men have been drawn to Christ and developed in Christ, their deployment for Christ will yield positive results, which will encourage the men to go out again and will encourage other men to join the fray.

These men are not the only individuals deployed by Jesus during the course of his ministry. As he prepared for the Last Supper, Jesus sent trained men to prepare the Passover *(Matthew 26:17-19)*. More importantly, as He prepared to ascend into Heaven after His resurrection, Jesus deployed all of his followers, including us, to go, teach, baptize, and teach *(Matthew 28:19-20)*.

The well-rounded men's ministry will be designed to provide opportunities for deployment. The men should operate ministries which are consistent with the vision of the church and which meet the needs of the church and community. At the author's church, the men's ministry deploys men in the following areas:

(1) Male Chorus and Male Ushers:

Men who have a desire to sing or usher are directed to the male chorus or male ushers. Once they become a part of one of these ministries they are encouraged to become involved in one of the evangelistic ministries of the Men's Ministry.

(2) Junior Laymen Ministry:

The men of this ministry provide guidance and companionship to boys in the church ages 8 through 18. This type of mentoring program is crucial to the development of boys into men.

(3) Community Outreach:

On every Friday night, the Men's Ministry, with the support of the other church members, provides dinner and a worship service to the homeless of our community. Between 70 and 100 individuals are transported to our Fellowship Hall, provided with a meal, and then with a message of salvation and hope.

(4)   Prison Ministry

A few years ago, the chaplain from a local prison contacted our church and requested assistance in providing worship services to the incarcerated men. That request was funneled from the Pastor to the Minister of Evangelism and Discipleship to the Men's Ministry. In response to this assignment, the Men's Ministry provided training (development) for 20 men who have been divided into teams, one of which is "sent out" every Thursday to provide a worship service at the local prison.

These represent the ministry opportunities that the Lord has developed in one local church. Depending upon the size of your church and the vision of your pastor, you may develop different ministries that meet different needs. Whatever the number or nature of the ministries, it is imperative that the men's ministry provide opportunities for men to serve in a significant capacity.

The men's ministry can also serve as a training ground and deployment depot for men to become active in ministries operated by the church at-large. At the author's church men from the Men's Ministry have become deacons, trustees, Christian Education leaders, teachers, and participants in the church choir. Some men have also been deployed as participants, teachers, lecturers and leaders in various denominational and interdenominational groups, such as state and national conventions.

The key to deployment, whether within the ministry, within the church, or outside of the church, is matching the right man with the right assignment. Discerning leaders analyze a man's gifts and talents and then deploy him in a position where those gifts and talents can be best utilized. This is a crucial aspect of deployment, as will be seen in the next chapter.

CHAPTER VIII

Every Man In His Place

(19) So Gideon, and the hundred men who were with him, came unto the outside of the camp in the beginning of the middle watch; and they had but newly set the watch: and they blew the trumpets, and break the pitchers that were in their hands. (20) And the three companies blew the trumpets, and break the pitchers, and held the lamps in their left hands, and the trumpets in their right hands to blow withal; and they cried, the sword of the LORD, and of Gideon. (21) And they stood every man in his place round about the camp; and all the host ran, and cried, and fled. [Judges 7:19-21]

In many respects the modern-day Christian church is dysfunctional. According to the eighty/twenty principle, twenty percent of the members of the church do eighty percent of the work. That is evidence of dysfunction. Often programs are started in the church but never finished. That is evidence of dysfunction. Church members who are called to work together cannot get along. That is evidence of dysfunction.

61

In the story of Gideon and his men found in Judges 7 we find a model of function in the church. Normally when we consider Gideon we remember he was the man God commanded to drastically reduce the number of men in his army. Perhaps you remember the story, found in *Judges 7:1-8.* Gideon had 32,000 men, and he was preparing to go into battle against 130,000 men. As he was preparing his battle plan God whispered in his ear: "You have too many men." God told Gideon to call all of his men together. As instructed, Gideon called his 32,000 men into the camp and simply said, "Anybody who wants to go home, go home." And the Bible says that 22,000 men left the camp, leaving 10,000 to fight the battle. (I have always wondered what would happen if in a modern day church, particularly during football season, the pastor took the pulpit on a Sunday morning and said, "Every man who does not want to be here, go home.")

So Gideon was left with 10,000 men. He went back to his study and was revising his battle plan when God whispered in his ear a second time and said, "You still have too many men." He instructed Gideon to take his men down to the river and watch them drink; God told Gideon to keep those who lapped like a dog, and dismiss those who drank from their knees. Out of the remaining 10,000 men, 9,700 drank the wrong way. Gideon sent them home and was left with 300 men. He started with 32,000, and he was outnumbered at that number. After Gideon's army was reduced to 300, God informed him he was ready for battle.

That is the story we remember when we recall Gideon. However, the story of Gideon and his men also provides us with an example of how leaders and followers in the church can work together for the glory of God. If we study the relationship between Gideon and his men, we can learn something about how we, as the modern-day church, can function better as we carry out the ministry God has left for us.

A GOD-CALLED LEADER

First of all, Gideon and his men were successful because Gideon was a God-called leader. Gideon was an unlikely candidate for leadership in his community. By his own testimony his family was the least family in town, and he was the least in his family. He was the least of the least, the left out and the leftover, but God called him to lead His people.

Gideon's ascent to leadership would be highly unlikely in the modern church. When we select leaders, often we look to the man who has the most education, who gives the most money, who has the most prestigious secular position, who dresses the nicest, who lives in the right neighborhood, or who drives the right car. Sometimes we simply select the man who talks the most.

We employ all types of criterion when we select leaders, usually to our detriment.

Gideon and his men were successful because they had a God-called leader. The lesson for us is apparent; if we desire a functioning church, a functioning ministry, or a functioning auxiliary, we need to make certain that we have a God-called leader.

There are three signs of a God-called leader. First, the leader that God calls will have a vision for the group God calls him to lead. (See Chapter II of this book). He will have a vision straight from God of where God wants the group to go. So, if a person seeks to be the leader of your group, a fair question is: "What is your vision?"

Second, a God-called leader has the ability to articulate his God-given vision so that people will understand. If you have a leader who has a vision, but cannot articulate the vision, he is not the one God called to be your leader. (Moses is no exception. His declaration that he could not speak is no indication that God would not have given him that ability when necessary to the fulfillment of Moses' mission.)

Third, a God-called leader has the ability to draw people to follow him. If a man has been president of an auxiliary for five years, and the auxiliary has the same number of members today that it had five years ago, it would be good for that man to examine whether God really called him to be the leader of that auxiliary, because when God's leader is in charge there is growth, there is expansion, there is fruit. Gideon and his men were successful because Gideon was a God-called leader.

A LEADER WITH CONFIRMED FAITH

Secondly, Gideon and his men were successful because they had a leader with confirmed faith. Leadership in the church requires faith, because when you lead God's people you will encounter mountains you cannot see around, and valleys you cannot see across. In these and other instances God's leader will be required to exercise some faith. As a consequence, God prepares his leaders by escorting them through circumstances that will increase their faith.

When he heard God's call, Gideon expressed disbelief. In fact, he proposed to give God a test *(Judges 6:36-40)*. Gideon took a piece of fleece, laid it out in his front yard, and told God that overnight He should demonstrate His omnipotence by making the fleece wet while keeping the ground dry. The next morning Gideon got up, went outside, looked in the front yard, and sure enough the fleece was wet and the ground was dry.

Now that would have been enough for me. That would have convinced me that I was dealing with God. But that was not enough for Gideon. Instead of accepting this miraculous sign Gideon proposed a second test. He laid a second piece of fleece in his front yard and challenged God this time to wet all of the ground while keeping the fleece dry (presumably a more difficult task). Gideon promised that if in the morning the fleece was dry and the ground was wet he would be convinced that he was dealing with God. Gideon went to bed that night, woke up the next morning, went outside, and sure enough the fleece was dry and the ground was wet. At that point Gideon declared his allegiance to God and his faith in God.

Gideon's conduct in this instance is often criticized. And, indeed, many of us would be offended if we extended a helping hand to a man in need and he questioned our sincerity or ability. The story of the fleece is significant because it demonstrates one of God's most endearing and enduring characteristics - He puts up with us. That is a part of being God.

God put up with Abraham when he lied about his wife's identity. He put up with David when he slept with

Bathsheba. He put up with Peter when he denied Jesus. He put up with Paul and Barnabas when they argued and feuded. He put up with the disciples when they ran out on Him, and if the truth be known every now and then He has had to put up with the author and the reader. God puts up with us.

And, what I have discovered is that God puts up with us not for our sake, but for His sake. God puts up with us so that we can become what God designed us to be and do what God designed us to do.

God puts up with us, and God put up with Gideon, even when Gideon had God doing foolish things — making fleece wet and making the ground dry. God put up with him because Gideon was God's called leader, and God was going to do whatever He had to do to make Gideon into what God had designed him to be.

EVERY MAN IN HIS PLACE

Gideon and his men were successful because they had a God-called leader. They were successful because they had a leader of confirmed faith. But finally, and most importantly, Gideon and his men were successful because, as verse 21 declares, "... every man stood in his place." That is a watchword for function. Confusion will be contained, progress will accelerate, and people will flourish when every man stands in his place. Four truths emanate from this seemingly simple thought.

Every Man Has A Place

First, the text suggests that every man has a place. God is no respecter of persons, and if He designed a place for Gideon, He designed a place for you. The Kingdom is not limited to preachers and deacons, to choir members and ushers — everybody in the church has a place. While it is true that in some churches those who do not carry an official title are made to feel inadequate and insignificant, the fact is if you are one of God's children, you are somebody, and God has designed a place for you. It does not matter how long you have been in the church, or how long you have been at the church; if you are a child of God, there is a place for you.

And, unlike football teams, there is no place on God's team on the sidelines. Everybody on this team is called to be on the field. God has a place for you to be active in His work. The church will never function like God designed it to function until we accept the fact that each member has a place.

Every Man Must Find His Place

Once you accept the proposition that every man has a place, next it is important that every man find his place. The most important question a man can ask is, "What must I do to be saved?" The second most important question a man can ask is, "Where is my place? Now that I have been saved, now that I have been washed in the blood and filled with the Holy Ghost, now Lord, where is my place?"

There are at least four ways to find your place:

(1) *Pray and ask God.*

"If any man lacks wisdom, let him ask God", James 1:5. Since God designed you for a place, it would be foolish for Him not to inform you of that place. God does not play hide-and-seek with us. If you want to find your place, get on your knees and ask God, "Where is my place?"

(2) *Study and search God's Word for examples of what other children of God have done.*

Although you are unique, it is likely that the place God has designed for you is similar to the place God designed for a forerunner. You may be a builder like Nehemiah, a wise counselor like Jethro, a

man of extraordinary faith like Abram, or a
leader like David.

(3) *Look around your church and see what is not getting done.*

If there is an empty place in your church and you are not doing anything, it may be (but not always) that you are the one God has designed to fill that place.

(4) *Seek the advice of your Pastor, other church leaders, and those in the church who have demonstrated a closeness with God.*

How you find your place is not nearly as important as actually finding it. I hope you grasp this truth if you do not grasp anything else - you will never experience true joy until you find your place. You will never receive all of what God has for you until you find your place. Until then, you are like a fish out of water, a square peg in a round hole, or in no hole at all. But once you find your place, you are on your way to being all that God designed you to be.

Every Man Must Accept His Place

Some of us find our place and reject it. Instead of accepting the place God has designed for us, many of us try to occupy the place we want for ourselves. I can give you a personal example. I wish I could sing. There is singing in my soul. There is singing in my heart. There is singing even in my throat, but somewhere between there and where it comes out, something bad happens. Given my lack of gift in that area, it would be foolish for me to demand to sing solos in the choir or to be the praise leader.

Irrespective of this irrefutable logic, there are those in the church who insist on filling roles, usually roles of prominence, to which they were not called and for which they are not qualified.

Martin Luther King. Jr. called it the "drum major syndrome". In every marching band there is one fellow who stands out in front. He is normally a tall, thin, good-looking fellow who wears a real big hat, carries a large baton, and marches by himself, stepping high, out in front of the band. That fellow is called the drum major. Every marching band ought to have one drum major, but only one.

How foolish would a marching band look with 100 drum majors; nobody playing instruments, just drum majors, marching up and down the field? Everybody cannot be the drum major. Somebody has to play the trumpet, somebody has to play the saxophone, somebody has to play the bass drum, and somebody has to be the guy who *pulls* the bass drum. He may seem insignificant, but without him the music would not be the same.

Here is a true story. Once there was a small laymen's group at a small church in Phoenix. The group, which was made up mostly of young professionals, met for Bible study every Tuesday night. One night a gentleman in his sixties who had recently joined the church came to the laymen's meeting. In fact, he came every Tuesday, and one day he raised his hand and asked to have a word. We will call him Bro. Smith. He commented on how he was inspired by the wisdom and articulate speech of the young men and then stunned the group by stating that he could barely read. He went on to ask the assistance of the young men in helping him improve his reading skills. The young men put him in touch with an adult literacy class, and Bro. Smith greatly improved his reading.

As the church was too small to afford a custodian, the young, professional, dignified, suit-wearing laymen were assigned the task of cleaning the church on a weekly basis. Being faithful men, they carried out the task, although not with overwhelming enthusiasm.

One Tuesday during the Laymen's meeting Bro. Smith raised his hand. He said, "Brothers, I understand you fellows clean the church before Sunday. I don't mean any disrespect, but I am a janitor by profession. I can't study the Bible like you, I can't teach the Bible like you, I don't wear fancy suits like you, but I know how to clean." He said, "It would make me feel good if you would let me come in on Saturday night and vacuum the floor of God's sanctuary. It would make me feel good if you would let me dust off the pulpit, so when the Pastor stands to preach the pulpit will sparkle. It would make me feel good if you would give me the honor of cleaning God's church on Saturday night, so that when God's people come in on Sunday morning, they will have a clean church to worship in." He concluded, "Would you give me the honor of cleaning God's church?" The author has it on good authority that the young professionals immediately granted unanimous consent.

That day, Bro. Smith, the one who had difficulty reading, taught a valuable lesson to the assembled professionals. Anything you do for God is significant and noteworthy, and we should use whatever gifts God has given us to glorify Him.

Different Places, Same Team

Although we have different places, we are all on the same team. Sometimes we get so infatuated with our place that we think our place is the best place, indeed, the only place. This attitude leads to infighting, jealousy, confusion, and dysfunction. We are in different places, but we are all on the same team. Deacons and Trustees, on the same team. Pastor and people, on the same team. Choir members and Ushers, on the same team. Laymen and Women's Auxiliary members, on the same team. We are not in a competition to see which choir can fill the choir stand to the fullest — we are on the same team.

I remember when the Chicago Bulls won their first championship by defeating the Lakers. What I remember most about that series is that, by its end, James Worthy, Magic Johnson, and Michael Cooper, all significant contributors for the Lakers, were on the bench, dressed in very nice suits, injured and out of place. And because Magic, Michael and Coop were on the bench, out of place, the Lakers lost.

I also remember the Bulls: Bill Cartwright, in the middle, playing defense, in his place; B.J. Armstrong, bringing the ball up, in his place; John Paxon, shooting long jump shots, in his place; Scottie Pippen, doing almost everything, in his place; Michael Jordan, doing everything, in his place. The Bulls had every man in his place, and the Bulls won. A clear-cut example that if you have every man in his place, you can be victorious.

The last thing I remember about the Bulls and the Lakers in that series is that each team had a captain. Magic was the Lakers' captain, and Michael was the Bull's captain. Like them, we who are on the Christian team have a Captain. King Jesus is our captain. You might wonder how Jesus got to be the captain of this team. He got to be captain because He stood in his place. He was King of kings and Lord of lords, but He was born in a manger instead of a mansion, because that was his place. He never had a place to lay His head, because that was His place. He was arrested in the garden of Gethsemane because that was His place. He carried His cross up Calvary's cruel hill because that was His place. They hung Him high and they stretched Him wide because that was His place. He hung His head and then He died because that was His place. They buried Him in a borrowed tomb because that was His place. He was there all night Friday, and all day Saturday, and all night

Saturday night, because that was His place. But early Sunday morning, when the women arrived to anoint His body, He was no longer there, because the grave was no longer His place. Death, where is thy sting? Grave, where is thy victory? And the Bible says that right now Jesus is at the right hand of the Father, making intercession for you and for me, IN HIS PLACE.

The Church as a whole and a Men's Ministry in particular must be in the business of helping men find the place God has designed for them and then encouraging men to stand in their respective places. In this manner we will fulfill God's plan for each of us and for the Church.

Conclusion

Where are the men? They are waiting to be drawn. They are waiting to be encouraged. They are coming forward with an expectation that the church will be relevant to their everyday lives. They desire to join other men in worship, fellowship, and service.

A local church men's ministry can be the depot where unsaved men and inactive men arrive. In order to be that depot, the ministry must have a clear understanding of purpose that is declared in its vision and reflected in its design and organization. That organizational chart should include mechanisms for drawing, developing, and deploying men. Through involvement in the ministry men sharpen each other; through prayer, and sometimes trial and error, men discover their gifts and the place God has designed for them. There is no greater joy than understanding your purpose and finding your place; the men's ministry is a great place for a man to come to this understanding.

It is our prayer that these humble thoughts will be of assistance, and that men's ministries will flourish throughout the land, all to the glory of God.